Tell Yourself This When You're Depressed

Also by The Quantum Shifter

The Truth of Reality
The Biggest Misconceptions About Manifestation
Why Isn't It Here Yet?
Manifest In Steps
Identity Shifting
One Decision Creates a New Reality
Self-Concept Selects Your Reality
It's Just a Reflection
Manifest Faster
Identity Shifting
I AM PERFECT
Embody a Wealth Identity
Mental Diet Mastery
Stop Spiraling While Manifesting
Emotional Mastery
Tell Yourself This When You're Depressed
Manifesting Money 101
Money From Nothing
You Are The Bank
Money Mindset For Single Moms
Your SP Loves You
Manifest A Celebrity
Have The Best Sex of Your Life
Lose Weight The Mental Way
Manifest Away "ADHD"
The Writer Everyone Reads
You Don't Need 3D Proof
Action Is Optional

The Positive Delusion
Cause and Effect Is a Lie
Objective Reality Is a Myth
Revision
Collapse & Command

TELL YOURSELF THIS WHEN YOU'RE DEPRESSED

Simple Words That Start to

Change Everything

The Quantum Shifter

IDENTITY PRESS

Connect with The Quantum Shifter

Website: www.TheQuantumShifter.com

Facebook: www.Facebook.com/TheQuantumShifter

ISBN: 978-1-972432-16-7

Published by Identity Press

These works were written over many years during the author's ongoing study of identity and reality creation.

They are now being published for the first time under the pen name *The Quantum Shifter*.

YOUR REALITY IS WHAT YOU SAY IT IS.

Contents

Before You Continue

This book will make the most sense if you are open to a simple idea: Your reality is not fixed. It is not happening to you. It is reflecting what you assume is true.

If you believe that reality is solid, unchangeable, and determined by circumstances, parts of this book may feel confusing or difficult to accept. And that's okay. You don't need to force yourself to believe anything. You can simply set this book down and return to it later, if and when it feels right.

But if something in you already senses that reality may not be what it seems—if you've noticed patterns that don't quite make logical sense—or if you've experienced moments where things shifted in ways you couldn't explain— then this book will likely feel familiar.

Not because it's teaching you something new, but because it's putting words to something you already know. Read it slowly. Let it land. And most importantly: Don't try to "do" anything. Just see what you notice.

A Letter from the Author

If you picked up this book, there's a reason. Maybe you've been feeling heavy lately. Maybe it's hard to care, hard to move, or hard to believe that things can ever feel different. I know that feeling – because I've lived there too.

For many years (in another lifetime), I experienced what the world calls depression. It colored everything. It convinced me that I was powerless and that life just *was* this way – lonely, empty, and dim. I didn't realize I was living inside a story that I kept unknowingly repeating.

No one told me that my words were creating that reality. No one told me that if I changed the story, the mirror would change too.

When I finally began speaking differently – even when I didn't believe it – I started to see light where there had only been dark. When I said *I am loved*, even though it felt like a lie, life slowly began reflecting love back to me. When I whispered *I matter*, I began noticing proof that I did.

That's what this book is about – remembering your authorship when it feels like you've lost it. You don't need to be positive all the time. You don't need to fix yourself. You only need to start saying new words, because those words become new worlds.

Let these pages meet you where you are. You can take your time. You can come back to one phrase again and again. Even one gentle thought is enough to begin turning the mirror toward peace.

You are not broken. You were never broken. You've always been the one with the pen in your hand.

With love,

The Quantum Shifter

How to Use This Book on Hard Days

Some days, you won't want to read. Some days, even turning a page feels too heavy. That's okay. You don't have to "keep up."

This book isn't meant to be read perfectly – it's meant to meet you where you are. On the days you can't do much, just pick one line. One sentence that feels kindest, truest, or easiest to say.

It could be *I am loved.* It could be *This moment will pass.* It could be *I am safe right now.* Say it once. Whisper it if you need to. That's enough.

You don't have to fix anything. You don't have to feel better instantly. You only have to speak a softer word than the one your mind is offering.

If all you can do today is breathe, breathe consciously. Each breath is an affirmation in itself: *I'm still here.*

When you're ready, you can flip to any page and let that message be your lifeline. There's no order. No pressure. Each chapter is a door back to yourself.

And when it feels impossible, remember – you don't need to climb out of the dark. You only need to call light by its name, one word at a time.

Introduction: The Moment You Forget Who You Are

Depression isn't just sadness. It's the moment you forget who you are.

You forget that you have any say. You forget that life still listens to you. You forget that the story running in your mind is *not* the truth – it's simply the reflection of what you've been rehearsing.

When you're depressed, your reality mirrors that loss of power. You start to see proof everywhere that no one cares, that nothing's changing, that you're alone. And the more you look at that reflection, the more convincing it becomes. You begin to mistake the mirror for the truth.

But here's the thing no one tells you: Depression doesn't take away your power. It just hides it behind your thoughts.

Even when you can't feel it, even when you don't believe it, you're still the one narrating reality. Every word you think or speak is still shaping what comes next.

For years, I lived in a reality called *major depression.* It felt endless, heavy, and hopeless. I believed the darkness, and the darkness kept proving me right. I didn't understand that the hopelessness I felt was just the echo of my own story repeating itself – not punishment, not failure, not destiny.

What I eventually realized was simple, but life-changing: If I could think my way into despair, I could speak my way out.

Not by forcing joy. Not by pretending. But by saying new words that carried even the smallest spark of truth.

The first phrase that began to shift everything for me was I *am loved.* I didn't feel loved when I said it. But I said it anyway.

Because I knew that my reality couldn't show me love until I started speaking love into it.

That's what this book is about – the power of small sentences spoken in the dark. You don't have to believe them yet. You don't have to feel better right away. You just have to say them –

because the moment you do, the mirror begins to move.

Each chapter in this book gives you a new sentence to tell yourself when you can't find your way out. Each one breaks a different part of the depressive loop — the story of being unloved, unseen, unsafe, or hopeless.

You'll see why depression isn't who you are. It's just a story that's been repeated too long. And when you start saying something new, that story begins to dissolve.

If you take anything from this book, let it be this: You are still the author. You are still the cause. And even when you forget, reality still listens.

Say the words. Let them echo. That's how the light gets back in.

"I Am Loved."

Chapter 1
"I Am Loved."

When you feel depressed, love seems like something that belongs to other people. You watch couples on the street, families laughing in restaurants, friends texting each other back – and it feels like life skipped you. It's not that you don't *want* to feel love. It's that your world has gone quiet, and the silence starts to sound like proof that you were never loved to begin with.

That's how the loop begins:

Thought: "No one cares about me."

Feeling: Lonely, unwanted.

Reflection: You stop hearing from people, or when you do, it feels hollow.

Evidence: "See? I knew it. Nobody really loves me."

It looks convincing, but it's only a mirror showing you the story you've been repeating. Reality isn't saying *you're unlovable* — it's echoing *your belief that love is gone.*

When you say **"I am loved,"** you interrupt the pattern. You're not forcing a fantasy; you're opening the door for life to reflect something new.

At first, it feels fake. You might even hear another thought whisper, *That's not true.* That's fine. Say it anyway. You're not debating the old story — you're replacing it.

Say it out loud. Whisper it. **"I am loved."**

Say it again while brushing your teeth, while lying in bed, while staring at the ceiling. You don't have to *feel* love yet. You're planting the frequency of it in the air.

And soon, you'll notice the mirror start to shift in small, almost invisible ways: - Someone texts you out of nowhere. - A stranger smiles at you in the grocery store. - Your pet leans against you for no reason. - You feel a tiny bit softer toward yourself.

These are not coincidences. They're confirmations. Reality always listens to what you call true.

"I am loved" rewrites your script at the deepest level. It tells the world, *I exist in a universe that cares about me.* It teaches your body to relax again. It reminds your mind that isolation was never the truth – only a temporary storyline.

The love that begins to show up won't always come as grand gestures. It might arrive quietly – a warm memory, a moment of sunlight through the window, a friend who finally reaches out. Don't overlook these moments. They are the proof you once said didn't exist.

When you keep saying **"I am loved,"** you stop waiting for love to appear and begin *being* the one who knows it's already here. And the mirror, as always, has no choice but to follow.

Chapter 1 – Integration

Supporting Affirmations

Try adding or rotating these with your main statement:

- "Love is already surrounding me."
- "I am open to being cared for."
- "Love keeps finding its way to me."

- "Every breath reminds me that love still exists for me."
- "It's safe to let love in."

Reflection Moments

You can write about or quietly think through any of these:

1. When in my past did I feel genuinely loved or supported, even briefly?
2. What does "being loved" look or feel like to me right now?
3. How might I treat myself today if I already believed I'm loved?

What to Notice

As you keep saying "I am loved," pay attention to small reflections that echo that truth:

- A stranger's kindness
- A memory that warms you unexpectedly
- Someone reaching out, even casually
- A softer inner tone toward yourself

These are confirmations, not coincidences.

Daily Practice

Once a day, place a hand over your heart and whisper, "*I am loved.*" Feel your heartbeat under your palm. Let that rhythm remind you that love is constant motion—already within you, always moving through you.

Anchor Reminder

Love has never left you; it was only waiting to be heard again.

Integration Notes

"I Matter."

Chapter 2
"I Matter."

When you've been depressed for a while, it can start to feel like you could disappear and the world wouldn't even notice. You might tell yourself, "*If I stopped showing up, would anyone really care?*" You might feel invisible — at work, in your relationships, even in your own home. And that invisibility begins to turn into a story: "*I don't matter.*"

That story doesn't stay in your head. It becomes the filter through which you experience life. People seem to forget you. Messages go unanswered. The world looks indifferent — but it isn't. It's only mirroring what you've been saying in silence.

When you say, **"I matter,"** you stop waiting for the world to prove your worth. You begin to prove it to yourself.

At first, the words might feel small. You might even think, "*That's not true — I haven't done anything special.*" But "I matter" isn't about accomplishment. It's not about what you've done. It's about remembering that your *existence* carries meaning.

There was never a test you had to pass to earn your place here. You already mattered the moment you arrived.

Say it gently, like you're reminding a friend: **"I matter."**

Say it when you feel unseen. Say it when you catch yourself apologizing for existing. Say it when your mind tries to list all the reasons you're not enough.

Because every time you speak it, you start creating a world that reflects it.

Here's what begins to happen when you anchor in *I matter*:

- People start responding differently — not because they changed, but because your energy did.
- You begin to take up more space without guilt.
- You make choices that honor your needs, not just your obligations.
- You stop over-explaining yourself.

- You start to see yourself again.

The feeling of mattering isn't something you earn through doing – it's something you *return* to through knowing.

And that knowing changes everything.

Even your smallest actions start carrying more weight. You walk differently. You speak differently. You stop needing validation to breathe.

When you say **"I matter,"** you're not convincing yourself of something new. You're remembering something ancient – something that's always been true, even when you forgot.

You are not a background character in your life. You are the author. You are the one who matters enough to write a new story.

Chapter 2 – "I Matter"

Supporting Affirmations

- "My presence makes a difference."
- "I belong here."
- "The world is better because I exist."
- "I add value just by being me."

- "I'm allowed to take up space."

Reflection Moments

1. Where in my life do I already make an impact, even if small?
2. What would I stop apologizing for if I knew I mattered?
3. How would I spend today if I treated my voice as important?

What to Notice

Notice when people respond to you, when someone smiles, thanks you, or listens. These small acknowledgments are reflections of the story *I Matter* taking form.

Daily Practice

Look into a mirror, meet your own eyes, and say: "*I matter.*" Hold eye contact until the words start to feel less strange and more true.

Anchor Reminder

You are not invisible—you are the reason light reflects at all.

Integration Notes

"I Am Not My
Thoughts."

Chapter 3

"I Am Not My Thoughts."

When you're depressed, your mind can feel like a cruel narrator. It comments on everything – what you did wrong, what you'll never have, why nothing will change. It tells stories that sound so convincing you stop questioning them. And over time, you start to believe that the voice in your head *is you*.

But it isn't.

You are the awareness that hears the voice. You are the one who notices the thoughts – not the thoughts themselves.

When you start saying **"I am not my thoughts,"** you begin to reclaim that space. It doesn't mean you'll never have dark thoughts again. It means you'll stop obeying them.

Most people live as if every thought is a command:

"I feel hopeless, so my situation must be hopeless." "I think I'm unworthy, so I must be." "I believe I'll never change, so I won't."

But thoughts are not laws. They're suggestions. And you don't have to accept every suggestion offered by the mind.

Try this: When a thought appears — "*I'll never get out of this*" — instead of arguing with it or trying to replace it immediately, just say quietly: **"That's just a thought."**

It's like watching a cloud drift by instead of climbing into it. No fighting. No fixing. Just recognition.

When you separate yourself from the noise, something miraculous happens: your power comes back. Because power can only exist in the one who observes, not the one who reacts.

Here's what you'll start noticing when you hold this truth:

- The thoughts still come, but they lose their grip.
- You stop spiraling so easily.
- You begin to choose what stays and what passes.

- You feel small pockets of peace, even in the middle of chaos.

You are not broken because you have dark thoughts. You are human. But you are also more than human – you are consciousness itself, aware of what's passing through.

Every time you say **"I am not my thoughts,"** you create distance between you and the noise. That distance is where freedom lives. It's the quiet space where new words can form – words like *I am loved, I matter, I am safe.*

You don't need to control the thoughts. You only need to stop becoming them.

Let the mind say what it will. You, the observer, get the final word.

Chapter 3 – "I Am Not My Thoughts"

Supporting Affirmations

- "I observe my thoughts; I don't obey them."
- "A thought is not a command."
- "Peace exists between my thoughts."

- "I can choose which words become my truth."

Reflection Moments

1. Which thought patterns feel the loudest right now?
2. How would my day change if I treated those thoughts as passing weather?
3. What calm statement could replace the harshest one?

What to Notice

Moments of silence, small pauses before reaction, easier breathing. Those are signs of distance forming between you and the noise.

Daily Practice

When a negative thought appears, breathe once and whisper: "*That's just a thought.*" Then add: "*I choose peace.*"

Anchor Reminder

You are the sky, not the storm.

INTEGRATION NOTES

"This Moment Will
Pass."

Chapter 4

"This Moment Will Pass."

When you're in the middle of a depressive wave, time stops moving. Every second feels the same – heavy, slow, and endless. You can't imagine feeling different tomorrow, because the weight of today feels permanent.

That's one of the cruelest tricks depression plays: it convinces you that what you feel right now is what you'll feel forever.

But that's never been true. No feeling has ever lasted forever. Not joy, not sadness, not fear, not peace. Everything moves – even when you can't feel it moving.

When you say, **"This moment will pass,"** you remind yourself of that truth. You break the illusion of permanence. You take away depression's greatest power: the lie that it's forever.

Think back for a second. There was a time when you felt this low before. And yet, here you are – still breathing, still showing up, still reading this page. That means every single storm you thought would destroy you has already passed. Every one.

You don't have to fix this moment. You only have to outlast it.

When you tell yourself *This moment will pass*, you loosen the knot of urgency that keeps the pain in place. You stop fighting the feeling and start allowing movement again. And the moment you stop resisting, it begins to dissolve on its own.

You might notice small shifts first – like the air feeling a little lighter, or a few seconds of silence between tears. That's the world turning again. That's time resuming its natural flow.

Depression tells you there's no point in waiting. But waiting is not failure. Waiting is power. Waiting is faith in disguise.

Every feeling has an expiration date – even this one. So breathe. Sit. Cry if you need to. But know that this moment is already on its way out.

Because you are not trapped in time. You are the one moving through it.

Say it softly whenever the darkness feels too close: **"This moment will pass."** Say it until it becomes a rhythm in your body. Because it always does.

Chapter 4 – "This Moment Will Pass"

Supporting Affirmations

- "Nothing lasts forever—not even this feeling."
- "Change is always happening for me."
- "Every breath moves me forward."
- "I'm allowed to outgrow this moment."

Reflection Moments

1. Recall a difficult time that eventually passed—what proof does that give you?
2. What feels permanent right now but might look different a week from today?
3. How does it feel to remember that movement is natural?

What to Notice

Shifts in light, temperature, timing, or emotion. Each is life reminding you: *Everything moves.*

Daily Practice

Touch something solid—desk, wall, bedframe—and repeat: "*This moment will pass.*" Let the stability remind you that time keeps carrying you.

Anchor Reminder

No season lasts forever; your sunrise is already on its way.

Integration Notes

"Life Is Still on My Side."

Chapter 5

"Life Is Still on My Side."

When you've been through too much – loss, disappointment, rejection, exhaustion – it starts to feel like life itself has turned against you. You stop expecting good things. You start waiting for the next hit. The world begins to look like an opponent instead of an ally.

You might think, "*Nothing ever works out for me.*" Or "*Every time I start to feel better, something ruins it.*" That belief quietly becomes the story that runs the show. And then the mirror – always obedient – begins to reflect exactly that.

But life has never been your enemy. It's only been your mirror. It's been showing you what you've been saying about it.

When you whisper, **"Life is still on my side,"** you start writing a new script. You're not denying what's happened. You're deciding what happens next.

Even in your lowest seasons, life has still been carrying you – through the air in your lungs, through people who show up just in time, through the quiet moments where you somehow made it one more day. You don't have to call it luck, or God, or the universe. You can just call it *life* – and it's been on your side the whole time.

Say it when things look unfair. Say it when you've just been let down again. Say it when you can't find proof that anything's improving: **"Life is still on my side."**

You'll feel a subtle shift – like the resistance softening, like your heart remembering how to trust. Because the truth is, life doesn't punish you. It reflects you. And when you begin to expect partnership instead of opposition, it starts rearranging itself to meet you there.

Small signs will appear – moments of relief, unexpected help, a little more lightness in your day. Not because something external changed first, but because you opened a crack in the wall.

When you start seeing life as for you, not against you, your nervous system begins to relax. Your guard lowers. And suddenly, solutions and support can reach you again.

This phrase is powerful because it brings you back to neutrality — the place where receiving becomes possible. You stop assuming you're cursed or forgotten and begin to realize you were never abandoned at all.

Every time you say **"Life is still on my side,"** you remind the mirror that you're ready to see evidence of support again. And the mirror always listens.

Chapter 5 — "Life Is Still on My Side"

Supporting Affirmations

- "Life supports me even when I can't see it."
- "Everything is working in my favor."
- "Help keeps finding me."
- "The universe and I are on the same team."

Reflection Moments

1. What small evidences of support have shown up recently?

2. How would I act today if I trusted life to have my back?
3. What could "life on my side" look like this week?

What to Notice

Tiny coincidences, offers of help, gentle timing—these are proof of partnership.

Daily Practice

Each morning say: "*Life is still on my side.*" Picture the day rearranging itself to meet that declaration.

Anchor Reminder

Life has never stopped choosing you.

Integration Notes

"I Am Safe Right Now."

Chapter 6

"I Am Safe Right Now."

Depression doesn't only live in your mind; it lives in your body. When you've been in survival mode for too long, the body forgets how to relax. Even small noises, bills, or texts can send a rush of tension through your chest. You might not even notice how often you're braced for impact — as if something bad could happen at any second.

That's what it feels like to lose your sense of safety. And without safety, peace can't stay for long.

Saying **"I am safe right now"** begins to rebuild that foundation. It doesn't mean pretending that everything is perfect. It means recognizing the truth of this moment: Right now, in this breath, you are safe enough to inhale and exhale. Your heart is still beating. You are still here.

The mind will try to argue: "*But what about tomorrow? What about the bills? What about everything that could go wrong?*" You don't have to answer those questions. You only have to return to the moment and say again, softly, **"I am safe right now."**

This sentence is a key. It brings you out of imagined danger and back into real time. It tells your body that the emergency has passed — even if your mind hasn't caught up yet.

Try saying it while you breathe slowly, or while you place a hand on your chest. Notice what happens: - The shoulders drop a little. - The air moves more easily. - The thoughts slow down just enough for you to think clearly again.

That's not denial. That's regulation. And regulation is what allows healing to happen.

When your body begins to feel safe, your reality follows. You start to draw in calmer people, gentler experiences, more helpful opportunities — because your energy no longer screams *danger*. You stop manifesting crisis and begin manifesting peace.

You don't need to fix your whole life to feel safe. You only need to claim this moment. One safe moment at a time becomes a safe hour. Safe hours become safe days. And eventually, safety becomes your identity.

Say it as often as you need to —in traffic, at night, during a panic wave, while paying bills. Each time you do, you're training your reality to match the feeling.

"I am safe right now." That's not wishful thinking. That's truth, re-established.

Chapter 6 — "I Am Safe Right Now"

Supporting Affirmations

- "I can breathe safely in this moment."
- "My body is allowed to relax."
- "I'm protected, supported, and present."
- "Peace belongs here."

Reflection Moments

1. What evidence of safety can I find right now?
2. How does my body feel when I tell it "You're safe"?
3. What routines or places help me feel calm?

What to Notice

Muscles loosening, slower thoughts, easier breath—your system returning to peace.

Daily Practice

Place one hand on your chest and one on your stomach. Say slowly: "*I am safe right now.*" Feel the body agree.

Anchor Reminder

Safety isn't found—it's remembered.

Integration Notes

“I Deserve Good
Things.”

Chapter 7

"I Deserve Good Things."

When you've lived in struggle for too long, peace can feel suspicious. Happiness can feel foreign. Even something as simple as someone offering to help can make you uncomfortable. You might think, "*I don't want to be a burden*," or "*People like me don't get things that easily*."

That quiet resistance is what keeps the cycle of struggle alive.

Depression often grows from a foundation of **unworthiness**—the belief that you don't deserve to feel good, be loved, have money, or experience ease. And because reality is always a mirror, it faithfully reflects that belief through experiences that seem to confirm it: - Things fall through. - Kind people fade away. - Good opportunities disappear before they reach you.

But the truth is, it's not that you aren't worthy. It's that you've been telling a story that says you're not.

And stories can change.

When you say **"I deserve good things,"** you're not being arrogant. You're being honest. You're remembering that your existence is reason enough to receive.

You were never meant to prove your worth through suffering. You were meant to remember it through awareness.

Say it like you're reclaiming territory that was always yours: **"I deserve good things."**

Say it when you catch yourself expecting disappointment. Say it when something kind happens and you feel the urge to minimize it. Say it when your mind whispers that it's selfish to want more.

Because each time you say it, you shift from rejection to reception. You stop repelling good things with guilt or disbelief and start creating a reality that reflects your worthiness.

At first, small blessings appear: - You find exactly what you needed on sale. - Someone compliments you, and you actually let it land. - A friend invites you somewhere, and you say yes instead of hiding.

Those are reflections of a changing identity. They're the world saying, "*We agree—you deserve this.*"

Receiving doesn't make you greedy. It makes you open. It allows energy to flow again.

The more you allow yourself to receive, the more you have to give. That's how generosity and abundance truly begin—not through guilt, but through overflow.

So the next time something good happens—big or small—don't shrink back. Don't wait for the other shoe to drop. Just breathe and say: **"I deserve this. I deserve good things."**

And reality will keep proving you right.

Chapter 7 — "I Deserve Good Things"

Supporting Affirmations

- "I am worthy of ease and joy."
- "Receiving is natural for me."
- "Good things are safe to keep."
- "I'm ready to let life be kind."

Reflection Moments

1. When was the last time I rejected something good out of guilt or fear?
2. How does it feel to imagine saying yes next time?
3. What's one "good thing" I can allow today?

What to Notice

Unexpected kindness, discounts, compliments, invitations—proof that goodness is arriving.

Daily Practice

Before bed, list three good things that found you today, however small. End with: "*I deserved every one of them.*"

Anchor Reminder

Receiving is your birthright, not a reward.

Integration Notes

"My Feelings Don't
Define Me."

Chapter 8

"My Feelings Don't Define Me."

Depression makes emotions feel absolute. When sadness comes, it doesn't feel like *a* feeling – it feels like *who you are.* When numbness sets in, it feels like the end of all joy. When anger or grief rise up, it feels like proof that you've failed at being "spiritual" or "positive."

But here's the truth: Feelings are weather, not climate. They pass through the sky of who you are – they don't become the sky itself.

When you start saying **"My feelings don't define me,"** you create distance between what's happening inside you and the identity you've attached to it. You stop saying "*I am depressed*" and begin saying "*I feel heavy right now.*" It seems like a small difference, but it's everything.

Because once you make that distinction, you remember that **you exist beyond the emotion.**

Imagine standing at the edge of the ocean, watching waves rise and crash. You don't mistake yourself for the water. You know the waves come and go – sometimes calm, sometimes violent – but they never change who you are standing on the shore. That's what your feelings are like. They rise. They crash. They retreat. And you remain.

When you believe that your feelings *are you*, you start living as if you have no choice. "I'm anxious, so I can't." "I'm sad, so I won't." But when you see feelings as visitors, you stop letting them make the rules in your house.

Try this practice: When an emotion comes up – maybe grief, sadness, frustration, or fear – instead of fighting it, name it and remind yourself: **"This is a feeling. It's not who I am."** Breathe. Let it exist without turning it into an identity.

Soon, the emotion begins to soften, not because you forced it away, but because you stopped feeding it with ownership.

You don't need to "fix" your feelings. You only need to stop worshipping them.

Your emotions are like the weather – signals, sensations, messages – but they don't decide the forecast for your entire life. You do.

Every time you remember **"My feelings don't define me,"** you return to stability. You stand in the identity that can feel everything without being consumed by anything. That's emotional freedom – not the absence of feeling, but the ability to remain yourself no matter what arises.

You can be sad and still loved. You can be angry and still good. You can feel lost and still be on your path. Because none of these feelings define you – they only pass through you.

And when they pass, what's left is truth. Calm. Clarity. You.

Chapter 8 – "My Feelings Don't Define Me"

Supporting Affirmations

- "I can feel without becoming."
- "Emotions move through; they don't make me."
- "I am steady beneath the waves."

- "Every feeling is temporary truth."

Reflection Moments

1. Which emotions feel strongest right now?
2. Can I describe them without judgment?
3. What remains constant underneath them?

What to Notice

Moments of neutrality, calm returning faster, fewer all-or-nothing thoughts.

Daily Practice

When emotion rises, name it: "*This is sadness.*" Then add: "*And I'm still me.*"

Anchor Reminder

You are the ground beneath every passing storm.

Integration Notes

"I'm Allowed to Feel
Better."

Chapter 9

"I'M ALLOWED TO FEEL BETTER."

One of the strangest things about depression is that when you finally start to feel even a little bit better, guilt often shows up first. You might think, "*How can I feel okay when nothing's fixed?*" or "*What if I let my guard down and everything crashes again?*" So you tense back up. You stop the momentum. You go quiet again.

That's not failure – it's habit. You've been living in survival mode for so long that peace feels suspicious. Joy feels undeserved. Hope feels risky.

And yet, healing can't begin until you give yourself permission to let those feelings in.

When you say **"I'm allowed to feel better,"** you open that door. You make peace with progress. You remind yourself that recovery isn't betrayal – it's alignment.

Sometimes, the fear of feeling better comes from identity. When you've identified as "the one who struggles," or "the one who's strong because they've survived so much," you subconsciously protect that story. You think, *If I get better, who will I be?* The answer is simple: you'll be free.

Freedom can feel unfamiliar at first, but that's okay. You're learning to let light back in without expecting the storm to return.

Say it softly: **"I'm allowed to feel better."** You don't have to justify it. You don't have to wait for a reason. You don't need permission from anyone else.

You're allowed to feel better even if: - You haven't "solved" everything yet. - Others in your life are still suffering. - You think you don't deserve relief. - It's been hard for so long that ease feels wrong.

The truth is, feeling better doesn't erase your past — it honors it. It says, *I made it through that. I can breathe now.*

And when you let yourself breathe, you start creating new evidence. You begin to attract new reflections — people, experiences, and opportunities that match your lighter energy.

Feeling better isn't the end of the journey. It's the beginning of new creation. It's the moment the mirror turns from showing your pain to showing your power.

So the next time guilt or fear whispers, "*You can't feel better yet*," answer with calm certainty: **"Yes, I can. I'm allowed to feel better."**

And every time you say it, your world agrees a little more.

Chapter 9 — "I'm Allowed to Feel Better"

Supporting Affirmations

- "Healing is safe for me."
- "I can relax into improvement."
- "Joy doesn't betray my past."
- "I have permission to thrive."

Reflection Moments

1. What guilt or fear comes up when I start to feel good?
2. What would life look like if feeling better

was my new normal?

3. How can I celebrate small relief today?

What to Notice

Tiny moments of laughter, lighter thoughts, peaceful pauses—these are progress, not luck.

Daily Practice

Each morning, before standing up, whisper: "*I'm allowed to feel better today.*" Let it guide your energy.

Anchor Reminder

Relief is not betrayal—it's evolution.

Integration Notes

"I Create What
Comes Next."

Chapter 10

"I Create What Comes Next."

At some point in every healing journey, you realize something powerful: you're not just surviving your story – you're writing it.

For so long, it felt like life was happening to you. Circumstances, people, emotions – all felt bigger than you, as if you were trapped inside a script someone else wrote. Depression deepened that illusion. It made you believe that you had no pen, no say, no power.

But every word you've spoken, every new sentence you've chosen – *I am loved, I matter, I am safe, I deserve good things* – has been you quietly taking the pen back.

When you say **"I create what comes next,"** you're claiming full authorship. You're not denying what happened before – you're ending its reign over what's to come.

You don't need to know *how* things will change. Creation doesn't start with a plan. It starts with a decision.

Every reality begins with a single thought accepted as true. Every chapter of your life begins with the words you speak next.

So take a deep breath. Notice what your mind wants to say about the future – maybe it whispers, "*It's going to be hard again*," or "*Things never last*." Don't fight those thoughts. Just recognize them as old drafts. Then speak a new one. **"I create what comes next."**

That statement cuts the cord between past and present. It tells your reality, *I'm ready for a new reflection*.

Creation doesn't require force. It doesn't require pretending that everything's perfect. It just requires willingness – the willingness to choose a different story, even when the old one still echoes.

And as you keep choosing, life responds. Maybe not overnight. Maybe not in fireworks. But subtly, steadily, the mirror begins to change. You'll notice small miracles – synchronicities, peaceful moments, kind words, opportunities you didn't expect. Those are the first paragraphs of your new story being written in real time.

You don't need permission to begin again. You already began the moment you started speaking differently.

You create what comes next every time you think, every time you speak, every time you decide who you are.

So the next time you start to wonder what the future holds, remember — it doesn't "hold" anything. It reflects *you.*

And you are the one who writes the ending.

Chapter 10 — "I Create What Comes Next"

Supporting Affirmations

- "My words shape my world."
- "I'm the author, not the audience."
- "Each thought is a brushstroke on tomorrow."
- "I choose the story I live."

Reflection Moments

1. What story have I been repeating that I'm ready to rewrite?
2. How do I want the next chapter of my life to feel?
3. What single word describes the energy I want to live from now?

What to Notice

Coincidences, new ideas, gentle motivation—proof that your creation power is active again.

Daily Practice

At night, before sleep, say: "*Tomorrow reflects what I decide tonight.*" Then think one peaceful thought as your last word of the day.

Anchor Reminder

Creation begins the moment you remember you're the writer.

Integration Notes

Conclusion — "You Were Never Powerless."

At the beginning of this book, you may have felt lost, heavy, and unseen. You may have believed your thoughts, emotions, and circumstances had more power than you did. But somewhere along the way, something began to s hift.

Maybe it happened quietly – a single line resonated, a breath felt deeper, a word felt truer than before. Maybe it was so subtle you almost missed it. That's how healing usually begins – not in lightning bolts, but in the soft decision to stop believing the lie of powerlessness.

You were never powerless. You just forgot that you were the one speaking reality into being.

Depression tells you that you're trapped inside a reflection you didn't choose. But now you know – you're never *inside* the reflection. You're standing in front of it, creating it. Even when the mirror showed pain, fear, or loneliness, it was only echoing what you unknowingly declared. And now, by choosing new words — *I am loved, I matter, I am safe, I deserve good things* — you've begun writing a different truth.

You've proven something extraordinary: You don't need proof before you speak power. You don't need to "earn" love or stability before declaring them yours. You only need to say it — and keep saying it — until reality catches up.

That's not pretending. That's remembering. That's mastery.

You've learned that:

- Feelings pass.
- Thoughts can be observed instead of obeyed.
- Safety and worth are identities, not circumstances.
- Life responds to your words, not your fears.

And if you ever forget again — because all humans do — you now have the map. Each statement in this book is a doorway back to your power. You can walk through any of them at any time.

You don't have to wait for motivation. You don't have to wait for the darkness to lift. You don't have to "deserve" better to start speaking better.

You simply decide that your voice matters — because it always has.

The truth is, the moment you picked up this book, you were already changing your story. You were already stepping into the identity of someone who creates on purpose. And from here, everything becomes lighter — not because life stops challenging you, but because you no longer forget who you are when it does.

So if you take nothing else from these pages, take this: You are loved. You matter. You are safe right now. You deserve good things. You are not your thoughts. You are not your feelings. You create what comes next.

You were never powerless — only powerful enough to believe that you were.

Now you remember. And from that remembrance, your new reality begins.

About The Author

The Quantum Shifter is the pen name of an Ivy-trained psychologist, researcher, and lecturer whose work explores the intersection of identity, consciousness, and reality creation. After completing advanced studies in psychology and spending years teaching and writing at the university level, she shifted her focus toward the deeper question that shaped her life's work:

How does identity create reality — and why does changing the story of who you are change the world you live in?

Her publications draw on decades of private research, academic inquiry, and experiential observation. Known for her clarity, precision, and deeply grounded approach, she writes about identity physics, timeline selection, self-concept, and the mechanics of reality in a way that is both accessible and transformative.

Although her academic background is traditional, her pen name reflects the evolution of her work — a nod to the moment she realized that consciousness itself is the most powerful instrument of change. The name stuck, and readers around the world now associate *The Quantum Shifter* with high-level insight, elegant simplicity, and rapid identity transformation.

She currently lives a quiet, contemplative life dedicated to writing, research, and teaching the principles of identity-based reality creation. Her books serve as distilled explorations of the concepts she has spent decades studying — written for readers who are ready to shift who they are, not just what they want.

www.ingramcontent.com/pod-product-compliance
Lightning Source LLC
Chambersburg PA
CBHW031331230926
51848CB00001B/189
* 9 7 8 1 9 7 2 4 3 2 1 6 7 *